HISTORIC MONTEREY

CALIFORNIA'S
Forgotten First Capital

by Eric Abrahamson

Produced for the California
Department of Parks and Recreation,
the City of Monterey, Monterey History
and Art Association, and the Community
Foundation for Monterey County
by Sequoia Communications,
Santa Barbara, California

Edited by
Joseph H. Engbeck, Jr. and Nicky Leach

Designed by Linda Trujillo

Type by Graphic Traffic,
Santa Barbara

First Printing 1989
Printed in Hong Kong
ISBN: 0-941925-04-8

ACKNOWLEDGEMENTS

This publication was a joint effort by several organizations. The editors would especially like to thank Donna Penwell and the Colton Hall Museum staff; Mary Wright and Paula Jones of the Monterey District Office of the California Department of Parks and Recreation; the entire staff of Monterey State Historic Park; and Jim Wright of the Monterey History and Art Association. Individuals who gave generously of their time include: Amelie Elkinton, Gary Brechini, Dr. J. S. Holliday, and Robert W. Reese. We would also like to thank Lawrence Dinnean at the Bancroft Library for his help with illustrations.

ILLUSTRATION CREDITS

Specially commissioned renderings of Old Monterey on the cover and p.7 by Olof Dahlstrand. Rendering of Monterey Custom House p.18 (top) by Olof Dahlstrand, courtesy Monterey History and Art Association. New photography of Monterey by John Huling on pages 2-3, 32 (bottom), 33 (top), 45 (top and bottom), 46 (top and bottom left, bottom right), 47 (top and bottom), and front flap. Path of History map on p.48 by Linda Trujillo.

Frank Balthis: 21, 41 (bottom right), 42 (bottom), inside back (middle and bottom), back cover; Bancroft Library: 1, 6 (bottom), 9, 10 (left), 11, 12 (top), 13, 14 (top), 15, 16, 17, 19 (top), 20 (bottom), 26 (bottom), 29 (top), 34 (top), 35 (top), 36, 37 (right), 38 (top right and bottom), 43 (top and middle), inside back (top); California Historical Society: 5, 26 (top); California Department of Parks and Recreation: 8 (top), 12 (bottom), 28 (bottom), 29 (bottom), 30 (bottom), 33 (middle); City of Monterey Public Library: 14 (bottom), 21 (top), 22, 34 (bottom), 35 (bottom), 37 (top, middle left, bottom left), 38 (top left), 39, 43 (bottom); Colton Hall Museum: 10 (top right), 19 (bottom), 27, 33 (bottom); Crocker Art Museum: 23; Russ Finley: 31; The Henry E. Huntington Library, San Marino, CA: 20 (top); Gary Moon: 8 (bottom), 30 (top), 40 (top and bottom), 41 (top), 42 (top), 44 (top and bottom), 46 (top right); Monterey History and Art Association: 28 (bottom); Joe Mora courtesy Monterey History and Art Association: 18 (bottom), 24-25; Franklin D. Roosevelt Library, Hyde Park, New York: 6 (top).

"On the 3rd of June, 1770, being the holy day of Pentecost, the whole of the officers of sea and land, and all the people, assembled on a bank at the foot of an oak, where we caused an altar to be erected, and the bells to be rung; We then chanted the Veni Creator, blessed the water; erected and blessed a grand cross, hoisted the royal standard, and chanted the first mass that was ever performed in this place; we afterwards sung the Salve to our Lady before an image of the most illustrious Virgin which occupied the altar; and at the same time I preached a sermon, concluding the whole with a Te Deum. After this the officers took possession of the country in the name of the King our Lord (whom God preserve). We then all dined together in a shady place on the beach; the whole ceremony being accompanied by many volleys and salutes by the troops and vessels."

Father Serra to
Father Palou, 1770

From a painting by L. Trousset, 1879.

INTRODUCTION

1846: THE YEAR OF DECISION

Sloat's Arrival in Monterey

Top: The U.S. squadron at anchor in Monterey Bay in 1847 by William Henry Meyers. Above: Commodore John Drake Sloat.

Late in the afternoon on July 2, 1846, Commodore John Drake Sloat of the United States Navy stood on the deck of the *Savannah* as it slid past Point Pinos off the coast of California and angled into the calm, blue waters of Monterey Bay. To his right, dark pine and cypress-covered hills rose up from the broken shore. To his left, the distant mountains above Año Nuevo were barely visible through the summer haze.

Above Sloat's head, the sails luffed in a light breeze. Men in the rigging called to each other as they brought the 54-gun flagship about and headed downwind towards two smaller American navy vessels already anchored quietly offshore. On the bluff overlooking the bay, he could see the cannons of El Castillo, the little Mexican fortress, facing out over the water. Just above the beach, the Custom House stood quiet, its flagpole curiously bare. Further inland, the red-tiled roofs and white adobe walls of Monterey stood warming in the afternoon sun. In the distance, along the left flank of the hills, an open parade ground and the bell tower of a chapel marked the site of the old Spanish presidio. Thousands of miles from Mexico City, this was the capital of Alta

Above: A view of Monterey as it looked in February 1835. From a watercolor by Olof Dahlstrand, 1989.

"The town lay directly before us, making a very pretty appearance, its houses being of white-washed adobe. . . . The red tiles, too, on the roofs contrasted well with the white sides and with the extreme greenness of the lawn, upon which the houses—about a hundred in number—were dotted about, here and there irregularly."

*Richard Henry Dana,
Two Years Before
the Mast*

6

California, Mexico's northernmost province.

Sloat was hardly pleased by what he saw. Sixty-eight years old, he suffered from a bad liver and rheumatism. His long, narrow face had been beaten by years of wind, sun and sea. Under his broad hat, his thick, stiff hair had receded giving him a high, Elizabethan forehead. Two months before, he had written a letter to the secretary of the navy asking to be relieved of his command. But long before his letter could reach Washington—travelling overland to the Gulf of Mexico, then by ship around Florida and up the eastern seaboard—rumors of war had reached him at Mazatlán.

War between the United States and Mexico had seemed inevitable ever since Texas declared its independence in 1836. The United States was obviously eager to expand its territory to the Pacific Ocean, and Mexico resented the aggressive and overbearing attitude of those American settlers and diplomats who seemed to believe that the United States had the natural right to take over Mexican soil. Some went so far as to claim that it was the "manifest destiny" of the United States to stretch from sea to shining sea.

For the last 10 years, every naval commander of the Pacific squadron had carried standing orders to occupy California in the event of war. But Sloat was not certain that his country was at war. Four years earlier, his predecessor, Commodore Thomas ap Catesby Jones, had sailed boldly into Monterey Bay, landed marines and ordered the surrender of El Castillo. He had pulled down the Mexican flag and raised the Stars and Stripes, only to learn from the American consul, Thomas Oliver Larkin, that in fact the two countries were not at war. Jones had embarrassed the President of the United States and disrupted negotiations with Mexico over the sale of California. Temporarily at least, the incident had cost Jones his command.

Sloat had no desire to make the same mistake. As his men stood by to drop anchor in the bay and he prepared to send an officer ashore with messages for the Mexican commander and the American consul, he was indeed a very reluctant conqueror. During the next few days, Sloat could not help feeling that he had entered onto a stage where all the actors seemed to know their parts and their lines, except him.

I dream of you,
I dream of you jumping,
Rabbit,
Jack rabbit,
Quail.

—Ohlone Hunting Song

Chapter 1

WATCHING FROM THE SHORE

Native Monterey and Early Spanish Exploration

As John Sloat rode up Alvarado Street on July 3, 1846, the history of the 76-year-old town of Monterey was evident in the faces of the people who greeted or watched him. Among them were the Californio families, descended from Spanish or Mexican soldiers and settlers. They now comprised the landed gentry. A handful of American and European expatriates—traders and merchants—also greeted Sloat or were introduced to him by the American consul.

Sloat may also have noticed the many Indians who were working around the homes and stables of the Californios. It is impossible now to tell what they thought of his arrival, but among them were the grand-children of Indians who had watched the first Spanish missionaries and soldiers arrive at Monterey in 1770.

The Spanish called them Costenos or "coast people," referring to nearly 40 different tribelets who had inhab-ited the land in and around San Francisco and Monterey Bays. Today, their descendants prefer the term Ohlone, which was once apparently the name of one of their villages on the San Francisco Peninsula. They had no universal name for themselves, but it seems clear that

Above: A sketch of an Indian attributed to José Cardero, a member of the 1791 Malaspina expedition. Left: An Indian mortar and pestle on exhibit in the Pacific House Visitor Center. Opposite: Ohlone Indians in full war dance regalia painted by Louis Choris in 1816.

Left: An Indian woman in Monterey by José Cardero. Above: Ohlone baskets displayed in Monterey earlier this century. Opposite: Ohlone Indians at Mission San Jose performing a traditional dance ceremony. From a lithograph published in a report by Dr. Georg Heinrich von Langsdorff, about 1806.

In 1841 a French visitor to California described an Ohlone dance ceremony as follows: "When dancing they are without clothes, merely adorning their heads with feathers and painting their faces and bodies. . . . Many of these dances are extremely licentious; others represent bear or deer hunts, or scenes from daily life such as starting off for war, or the death hunt."

they lived together in this part of the world for more than a thousand years.

The Ohlone followed the cycle of the seasons as they hunted and gathered food, married and bore children, prayed and offered gifts to the sun and the spirits of a variety of living things. Linguistic and physical evidence suggests that they moved into the Monterey Bay area somewhere between 500 B.C. and 500 A.D., merging with or displacing an older people, the Esselens, who had inhabited the area for nearly 2,500 years.

Once in place, however, the Ohlone settled in so permanently that between the Golden Gate and Point Sur eight different languages evolved, as distinct from each other as French and Spanish. Within those languages, there were also various dialects. In the Monterey area in 1770, for example, approximately 800 Ohlone lived in a number of tribelets along the peninsula and the lower parts of the Carmel and Salinas Rivers.

Their main village was known as Rumsen and this is how we refer to them today.

Among them, the men went naked or, on cold mornings, smeared mud on their bodies for warmth. A few wore long beards, but many picked the whiskers from their faces with pairs of mussel shells or wooden tweezers. Women wore two skirts, one in front and one behind, made of fur or grass. Frequently they tattooed their faces with dots and lines.

Like other Ohlone, the Rumsen lived off the land and sea, eating salmon and steelhead, mussels and abalone, quail and geese, rabbit and bear, as well as a host of other mammals, birds, shellfish, reptiles, and plants. They hunted game with bows and arrows, fish with nets, small game with traps, and birds with nets, traps, and bolas. Animals of all kinds were so abundant that Europeans arriving in the 18th century were astonished.

The Ohlone had both permanent and temporary village sites. They moved with the seasons, building homes framed with wooden poles and thatched with tules or brush. The homes surrounded a large assembly hut, which was used for a wide variety of ceremonial and political purposes.

They were a relatively peaceful people, but wars were fought between the tribelets, often over territorial infringements. In the Monterey area, the Rumsen fought with both the Esselen to the south and the Salinan to the east. Prisoners were rarely taken. The victors might decapitate the vanquished and take scalps, and parade their trophies on poles. Such violence was rare, however, and most conflicts were resolved with minimal fighting. Foes one day could become trading partners the next.

In fact, the Ohlone way of life was characterized by remarkable stability. Each group of people knew its land so well that individual trees and animals had names. Almost nothing in the Ohlone world was unfamiliar.

The sight of the first Spanish ship off the coast of Monterey Bay, with its great white sails unfurled, riding the tide like some enormous sea bird, must have been awe-inspiring to the Rumsen. In 1542, two ships captained by Juan Rodriguez Cabríllo, a Portuguese navigator sailing under the Spanish flag, passed Point Pinos and were probably seen from the shore. This was perhaps the Ohlone's first contact, albeit at a distance, with Europeans.

Cabrillo was exploring the California coast. Having narrowly escaped a storm farther out to sea, he was afraid to go ashore anywhere near Monterey because of the weather. Nevertheless, he claimed this entire coast for the King of Spain and named the bay Bahía de los Pinos, calling its southern point Cabo de Pinos, the Cape of Pines.

Sixty years later, the Rumsen watched in some awe as another wind-driven ship brought Spanish explorer Sebastián Vizcaíno into Monterey Bay. Vizcaíno was looking for a safe harbor for Spanish galleons travelling the Pacific and trading in the Philippines and the Far East. Coming ashore with his men and Carmelite friars, Vizcaíno once again claimed the land for Spain. Under the boughs of a great oak tree that grew close to the beach immediately west of where Fisherman's Wharf is today, the friars conducted mass on December 16, 1602. Vizcaíno named the bay after his patron, the Count of Monterey, who was the viceroy of New Spain.

The Rumsen watched Vizcaíno and his men as they spent the next several days repairing ships and exploring. South of the Punta de Pinos, Vizcaíno discovered a small river that he named El Rio de Carmelo after the friars. Then, on January 3, he and his men went back to sea in their ship and soon disappeared over the horizon.

For generations the Rumsen told neighboring tribes of the bearded men who had visited them. But 168 winters would come and go before such visitors would come ashore again. When they did return, the Rumsen were the first to feel the impact of their presence. And what happened to them at Monterey soon began to happen to other Northern California coastal Indian groups—cataclysmic changes that would permanently destroy age-old ways of life for Indian people throughout California and the West.

*The missions and new
establishments of the
Californias are still very
much in their infancy...
It will require a prudent
man...to plant, preserve
and root good order there.*

—Viceroy Bucareli to
Governor de Neve.
September 30, 1774

Chapter 2

TRANSPLANTING A WAY OF LIFE

The Spanish in California

The colonization of California by missionaries and
soldiers has been described as the dream of a madman.
At various times, José de Gálvez, Visitador-General of
New Spain, who oversaw the formation of the Sacred
Expedition to Alta California, suffered from strange
delusions. On occasion he told people he was God.
Once, in order to subdue Indians in Arizona, he proposed importing 600 Guatemalan apes and outfitting
them as soldiers to fight for the glory of Spain. These
breakdowns, however, were temporary and came after
he succeeded in launching the expedition northward
into Alta California. Overall, Galvez was one of the
most brilliant, able, and effective administrators New
Spain ever had.

From the time of Balboa's discovery of the Pacific in
1513, Spain had asserted its dominion over the ocean
and its American coasts. But after several decades of
remarkable exploration, during which Spanish ships
traced the coastline of the Americas from Newfound-
land south to the Strait of Magellan and north again
as far as Oregon, the Spanish had concentrated on

*Top left: José
de Gálvez, Visitador-
General of New Spain.
Left: Father Junípero
Serra, "Father of the
California Missions."
Above: A view of the
Monterey Presidio
by José Cardero.*

12

Vista del Presidio de Monte Rey.

developing Mexico and Latin America. Little had been done to colonize north of the southernmost tip of Baja California.

Then in the mid-18th century, Charles III became King of Spain. Under Charles, a rejuvenation of the Spanish Empire took place. Concerned by reports of Russian encroachment along the Pacific coast between 1741 and 1765, Charles encouraged Gálvez's plans for colonial expansion in North America into the Great Plains, the Louisiana territory, and along the coast of Alta California. The king was also moved by Gálvez's reminder that it was his duty to the Church to promote the conversion of the Indians in the New World.

Gold, the glory of God, and personal honor were extremely powerful influences on Spanish men in the 18th century. Father Junipero Serra, for example, was overjoyed when Gálvez picked him to oversee the development of missions in Alta California because he hoped to be killed and martyred there. Captain Gaspar de Portolá was chosen by Gálvez to lead the expedition to Monterey and oversee the establishment of a mission and fortress there. Portolá had misgivings about the

entire scheme, but he nevertheless obeyed his orders, despite severe hardships.

Indeed, Portolá and Serra were among the minority of those who survived the trip north to San Diego and Monterey. More than half of the 300 men who left Loreto in Baja California in March of 1769 died on the way north. On their first night in San Diego, the survivors gathered around a campfire and debated whether or not they should abandon the idea of continuing to Monterey. In the end, Portolá decided to take all those who could stand the journey and leave Serra at San Diego with just enough men to care for the sick.

Portolá started northward on July 14, planning to rendezvous with one of his ships in Monterey Bay. After two and a half months of hard travel, he and his men followed the Salinas River (mistaking it for the Carmel) down to the shore of Monterey Bay. To their surprise, they found none of the landmarks so glowingly described by Vizcaíno, and therefore did not believe they had found Monterey Bay. Punta de Pinos appeared to the south instead of the north, and there was no supply ship waiting offshore.

Plaza del Presidio de Monte – Rey

Confused and discouraged, they discussed whether they should continue. Vizcaíno's glowing description of Monterey in winter hardly matched the place Portolá and his men now found in summer. As the captain said to his men: "The Carmel River is only a creek, what should be a port is only a little bay."

Portolá and his men continued north. In the first week of November they discovered San Francisco Bay, which had apparently eluded all previous explorers. But finding no ship waiting, they were only further discouraged. In despair, they returned south. On November 11, they camped again on the shores of Monterey Bay, but still did not recognize it. They erected two crosses: one at the mouth of the Carmel River, and one overlooking the beach, a mile east of Monterey. At the foot of each cross, they buried a note telling their story, in case the ship should arrive. Then, without further delay, they headed south for San Diego.

By the time he reached San Diego and talked with Father Serra, Portolá had realized his mistake. Serra urged him to return to Monterey as soon as possible. But in San Diego conditions had hardly improved. Father Serra had founded Mission San Diego de Alcala, but had not won a single convert. Months had passed with no fresh supplies from Mexico.

Above: The only known sketch of the inside of the Monterey Presidio was made by José Cardero.
Right: The mission had already moved to Carmel when Cardero sketched this view of it.

Portolá believed the expedition should be abandoned. Too many lives were at risk. His judgment was based on prudence and reason. But Serra exhorted him to have faith, to go forward despite the circumstances. He, in fact, welcomed death. For years afterward, other priests and other soldiers would have similar arguments as both the Church and the government struggled to colonize California.

At last, Serra persuaded Portolá to wait until the feast of St. Joseph on March 19. Miraculously, on the afternoon of the 19th, the sails of the *San Antonio,* which was carrying fresh supplies, were sighted. With hope renewed, Portolá sent Father Serra and a party of soldiers under Lieutenant Pedro Fages to Monterey aboard the *San Antonio* while he and a group of men set out once again for Monterey by land.

This time, there was no mistaking Vizcaíno's famous bay. Portolá arrived on May 23 and a week later, the *San Antonio* arrived by sea—dramatic evidence of how difficult the northbound trip was, against the prevailing winds, up the California coast. On June 3, 1770, Father Serra conducted mass under the shade of Vizcaíno's oak tree at the water's edge and proclaimed the founding of the mission and presidio of San Carlos Borroméo de Monterey—six years before the American Revolution, 19 years before the French Revolution and the rise of Napoleon, and 78 years before the discovery of gold in the American River.

King Charles III could now claim authoritative rule over lands from Madrid to Argentina to the Philippines, and to Saint Augustine, Santa Fe, San Antonio, and Monterey in North America. But his rule was to prove short-lived and Monterey was never replaced as the northernmost of the Spanish Empire's provincial capitals in the New World.

As head of the military expedition, Portolá became California's first governor. Immediately, he began the construction of a presidio to occupy and defend the port from "the atrocities of the Russians, who were about to invade us." Built on a rise above a small inlet or *estero,* the presidio was at first a crude collection of huts enclosed by a wooden palisade. One of the huts was dedicated as a temporary church, and here Father Serra, as head of the community of Franciscans, began the work of converting the Rumsen, and then other groups of Ohlone who came out of curiosity or were rounded up by soldiers.

On July 9, Portolá sailed for Mexico, glad to leave the business of colonizing in the hands of Lieutenant Fages. But despite Portolá's departure, the battle of wills between soldier and priest continued. As the months rolled by, Fages opposed Father Serra's desire to begin founding more missions. He argued against spreading his soldiers and resources too thinly.

In the meantime, life in Monterey was tenuous at best. Morale was low and there was very little food—much of what there was being provided by the Rumsen. For their part, the Indians came voluntarily at first. Once they had agreed to be baptized, however, the priests, believing it was their duty to protect their new flock, virtually imprisoned them. In the mission, the Indian way of life was repressed. Many died of diseases brought by the Spanish: measles, smallpox, diphtheria, and syphilis.

Bored and far from home, Fages' soldiers frequently took advantage of the Indian women at the mission. To remove the Indians from the idle soldiers, Father Serra moved the church from the presidio to the Carmel Valley in the summer of 1771. That summer, also, fresh supplies and soldiers along with 10 more priests arrived in Monterey by ship. With this newly arrived help, Serra overcame the objections of Fages and managed to establish three new missions, although he was frustrated in his efforts to start still more.

Misión del Carmelo de Monterey

JEAN FRANÇOIS GALAUP
DE LA PÉROUSE.
Chef d'Escadre des Armées Navales born at Alby in 1741.

In 1776, Father Serra managed to found the Mission of Saint Francis of Asis on the shores of San Francisco Bay. That year also, a new governor, Felipe de Neve, was appointed to rule over both Baja and Alta California with his capital in Monterey. Intelligent, well-educated and an able administrator, in five brief but important years, de Neve oversaw the creation of more settlements, the implementation of a code of laws known as the Reglamento, and the awarding of the first land grants.

Father Junipero Serra died in 1784. In 14 years, he had founded nine of the 21 Franciscan missions that were eventually established in Alta California. He was buried in Mission San Carlos de Borroméo, the mission he had founded beside the Carmel River.

Thus, the first, and in many ways the most significant, phase of Spanish imperial expansion in Alta California came to an effective end. The work of the missions would go on, governors would come and go for 38 more years, but already Spain was losing its ability to control or even help the small settlements in California.

Throughout the 1790s and the early 1800s, the Pacific coast was visited by representatives of a number of other nations who had heard of California and wanted to know more. In 1786, for example, a European nobleman, the Comte de La Pérouse, arrived in Monterey. He was engaged in a global voyage of scientific exploration for the French government, and his visit was the social highlight of the decade as Governor Fages and his wife hosted a party for the visiting dignitaries. La Pérouse kept an extensive journal of his voyage and was one of the first Europeans or Americans to remark that California cried out for development, but that development was unlikely to occur under Spanish rule. In 1792, George Vancouver, a British commissioner, visited Monterey on a tour of the Pacific coast. He too was surprised at how poorly fortified and crudely constructed the presidio at Monterey was.

Above: The Comte de La Pérouse visited Monterey in 1786, the first foreign visitor to enter Spanish California. Right: George Vancouver brought a British expedition to California and the Pacific Northwest in 1792. Opposite: A member of the de La Pérouse expedition made this sketch of the reception ceremonies at Mission San Carlos Borromeo. The oil painting made from this sketch now hangs in the Museo Naval, Madrid, Spain.

Meanwhile, in Europe and on the east coast of North America, democratic ideas and ideals were spreading rapidly, sparking revolution first in the British colonies and then in France. With the rise of Napoleon and the ensuing European power struggles, Spain could only feebly protect her empire. In Latin America, revolts began in Peru as early as 1780, but were put down by royalist sympathizers. Then in 1808, Napoleon placed his brother Joseph, a Frenchman, on the throne of Spain. This act enraged Spanish-American patriots and took away all royal legitimacy. It made possible a broader rebellion against the Crown.

A decade of power struggles began in Central and South America though these politics were largely ignored by Spanish settlers in California. They noticed only the absence of supply ships and the lack of government attention. On one occasion late in the decade, however, the citizens of Monterey were made cruelly aware of the revolutionary turmoil abroad.

Hippolyte de Bouchard was the commander of two vessels under the flag of the newly independent Argentina. In November 1818, he sailed into Monterey, and after firing upon El Castillo sent a message ashore demanding the surrender of the city and "all the furniture and other belongings of the King."

Governor Pablo Vicente de Solá sent a defiant reply to Bouchard, but had no means or men to back his brave words. When Bouchard and his men landed, the governor and most of Monterey's residents fled from the city. Called a pirate by some and a revolutionary patriot by others, Bouchard and his men pulled down the Spanish flag and ransacked and burned much of Monterey. On December 1, after loading as much livestock and other food as they could take, the two ships left as quickly as they had come.

Monterey recovered. The flag of Spain was raised once again, and El Castillo, the harbor defense installation on the hill above the bay, was refurbished and improved. But the days of the Spanish Empire were numbered. The spirit of independence was moving through all of the Americas and stirring the hearts of Latin American colonists like a fresh breeze at sea begins to fill the sails of a ship becalmed in the doldrums. It would not be long before a new flag would fly at Monterey.

*I have never been in a
community that rivals
Monterey in its spirit
of hospitality.*

—Walter Colton, First Alcalde,
Monterey, 1846-1849

Chapter 3

ALTA CALIFORNIA: A QUIET, DISTANT SHORE
The Mexican Era in California

Mexico gained its independence from Spain in the summer of 1821. For a year the new country was ruled by Emperor Augustín de Iturbide, who was then deposed. Two years later, in 1824, Mexico became a republic composed of 19 states. The distant province of California, however, remained a territory.

When news of independence reached California in March of 1822, few of the colonials could believe it. Only a few weeks earlier, Governor Pablo Vicente de Solá had confidently written to a peer that independence was "a dream," that the Spanish Empire was "immortal." Now, he and his officers had to decide what California should do. Solá convened a meeting in Monterey of officers from the various presidios. Father Vicente Francisco de Sarria represented the missions. At length, like good and dutiful soldiers, they swore their allegiance to the new government and proclaimed the news in the streets of Monterey.

Top left: A pencil sketch of the Custom House as it looked in the spring of 1846, as rendered by Olof Dahlstrand. Left: The famous Monterey-based artist Jo Mora sketched and painted many scenes of Californio life. Above: Monterey in 1827 as painted by William Smyth. Right: A typical Californio scene in Monterey.

Five months passed before any official from the Mexican government came to take actual possession of California. Then one afternoon near the end of September, a ship appeared in the bay flying a green, white, and red flag with an emblem in the center showing an eagle holding a snake. In the days that followed, that flag was raised in Monterey amidst shouts of "Viva la Independencia Mejicana." The celebration that followed included foot races, feasting, and a grand ball.

Solá continued as governor of Alta California, with his capitol in Monterey. Under Mexican rule, the first California legislature met in Monterey on November 9, 1822. It included six representatives from throughout the proposed state. After the fall of Augustín in Mexico City, even more democratic reforms followed, one of the most important being a new constitution that guaranteed all the nation's citizens, including Indians, political and racial equality and the right to vote and hold office—this at a time when neither blacks nor Indians were recognized as citizens in the United States.

Above: Trying Out Tallow, Monterey, *by William Rich Hutton about 1830. Below: An 1854 lithograph of* Carmel Mission *by Cyrille Pierre Théodore Laplace from an original painting by François Edmond Pârís in 1839.*

Most important for California, Mexico's new leaders, hoping to create a strong and dynamic economy, liberalized foreign trade restrictions. Since the turn of the 19th century, American, Russian and British ships had sailed along the coast of California hunting sea otters for their pelts. Spanish law had made it illegal for Californians to trade with these ships, though the law was frequently circumvented or ignored. By the time of Mexican independence, however, the otter population had diminished substantially. American whaling ships began to ply the waters off the coast of California instead. And under the new trade laws, British and Yankee merchants began to cultivate a whole new industry in skins—this time in cattle hides.

Governed by the padres, the California missions had grown reasonably wealthy since 1770, raising thousands of head of cattle and growing acres and acres of grain. Settlers, borrowing from the mission herds, had also begun to raise cattle on land granted to them by the government. Beyond a certain point, the cattle were not especially valuable for meat; there was virtually no way to export it to a population center without it spoiling. What was valuable to Americans and Europeans during the middle of the Industrial Revolution were the hides, and tallow that could be made from the animal's fat. Shipped in great quantities, the hides provided the raw material that newly created factories in England and on the East Coast used to make shoes, boots, and other leather goods. The tallow was used to make candles.

The first merchants to exploit the potential of the California hide trade were British: Hugh McCulloch and William Edward Petty Hartnell. The two men arrived in Monterey in 1822 and began a partnership known to the Hispanic locals as "Macala and Arnel." Within a matter of weeks, however, competition arrived in the person of William A. Gale, a Boston trader representing Bryant, Sturgis Co. These two operations dominated the hide and tallow trade throughout the 1820s. Bryant, Sturgis Co. alone shipped close to half a million cattle hides to American shoe factories in the 1820s and 1830s.

The advent of trade brought a number of foreigners to Monterey, many of whom would play a prominent role in the city's and the state's history. In 1823, Captain John R. Cooper arrived on board the American schooner *Rover,* sold his ship to Governor Luis Arguello, but remained as ship's captain. Later, as a resident of Monterey, Cooper became a merchant and convinced his half brother, Thomas Oliver Larkin, to join him in California. In 1824, David Spence, an Englishman, arrived to work as an assistant for William Hartnell, and a young Spanish Basque man named José Amesti arrived aboard the trading ship *Panther.*

From top: William Edward Petty Hartnell; Thomas Oliver Larkin; and Larkin House as it looks today.

Most of these foreigners were welcomed in California on the condition that they be baptized into the Catholic faith. Some eventually took Spanish names and married into the leading local families—the *gente de razón*. The presence of these foreigners, combined with the increasing infiltration of products of the Industrial Revolution and the proliferation of democratic ideals espoused by the new government in Mexico, planted the seeds of a new society in Monterey and California. Among the leaders of this new community were a number of young men, "Californios," the offspring of Spanish settlers, who had been born and raised on the Pacific Coast. In Monterey, Mariano Vallejo, Juan Bautista Alvarado and José Castro were perhaps the most prominent.

The new ideas increasingly conflicted with the mission system and the Church. In 1831, 23-year-old Vallejo obtained a number of liberal books from a German merchant, several of which had been banned by the Church. He shared them with his friends Alvarado and Castro. When Vallejo's sister reported them, Vallejo and his friends were ordered to turn over the books, go to confession and say penance. To the horror of their parents, the young men refused and were unofficially excommunicated from the Church.

Vallejo, Castro, and Alvarado represented a whole class of Californios who had always regarded the missions with a mixture of awe, envy and skepticism. Indeed, there was increasing resistance to the power of the Catholic Church. In Mexico and California, this movement became a campaign to secularize the missions.

As originally conceived, the missions were supposed to convert the native California peoples, teach them to farm, and eventually to govern themselves, leaving the padres free to found new missions elsewhere. But by the 1820s, it was apparent that the mission fathers had made little progress in moving toward self-determination for the Indians. Moreover, the *gente de razón* increasingly coveted the vast acreage and great herds of animals controlled by the padres.

The "new liberal" Californios: Vallejo, Alvarado, and Castro. Their protests about the power and wealth of the California missions helped bring about secularization of the missions in the mid 1830s. Opposite: A romantic view of Californio life, The Fandango, *as painted by Charles Nahl in 1873.*

These factors led to the secularization of the missions in the mid-1830s. By Governor José Figueroa's proclamation of August 9, 1834, the mission lands were to be distributed half to Indians and half to other Californios and settlers. The process was to take three years. Practically speaking, however, most mission assets fell into the hands of a powerful few. Many of the recipients were friends of Juan Bautista Alvarado, who in 1836 became governor following Figueroa's death.

With the acquisition of these lands and herds, came the creation of an upper class of native-born Californios. The Californios expressed their loyalty to the traditions and politics of Spain and Mexico, but increasingly they were influenced by the ideas and actions of the foreigners among them, and by a growing sense of native pride.

In the late 1820s and 1830s, Monterey grew beyond the immediate vicinity of the old presidio. In 1827, reflecting the increasing importance of foreign trade, the first part of the present-day Custom House was built overlooking the beach. Moreover, many prominent citizens began to erect substantial adobes for use as private residences. When Boston-bred, Harvard-educated, Richard Henry Dana visited as a common sailor on board the *Pilgrim* in 1835, he saw about a hundred houses, mostly one-story adobe cottages, scattered about on a broad, green shelf of land. In his book *Two Years Before the Mast,* Dana described the town as "the pleasantest and most civilized-looking place in California."

Foremost among the houses of Monterey was the home of Thomas Oliver Larkin, a two-story adobe that combined Spanish and New England architectural styles to fit available materials and conditions in Monterey. The house pioneered a style in homebuilding that came to be known as the "Monterey" style. Larkin had come to Monterey from Boston in 1832 to help his half brother, John Rogers Cooper, with his business. He quickly became the area's leading merchant, and then in the 1840s, American consul and special agent. His wife, Rachel Hobson Holmes, was the first American woman to take up residence in California.

Above and opposite: These Californio figures were meticulously researched and painted by Jo Mora. The originals now hang in Casa Serrano in Monterey. Top, from left: Vaquero, Franciscan Monk, Neophyte Body Servant, and Neophyte Woman. Above, from left: Portolá's Dragoons and a Catalonian Volunteer.

By the early 1840s, British, French, and American naval vessels were frequent visitors to Monterey Bay, and an ever-increasing number of foreigners were arriving either by ship or overland to settle. When Texas declared its independence from Mexico in 1836, Californios received the news with ambivalence. They too sometimes yearned for independence. At times, however, they worried about unlimited Yankee immigration and the threat of eventual domination. Their fears were not put to rest in October of 1842 when two American navy vessels sailed into Monterey harbor and anchored.

Commodore Thomas ap Catesby Jones commanded the American naval forces in the Pacific. Like Commodore Sloat four years later, Jones carried standing orders to occupy Mexico's California ports in the event of war between the United States and Mexico. Anchored in Peru in early September 1842, Jones received word that led him to believe war had been or would be declared within days. He immediately set sail for California.

Just outside Monterey Bay on October 18, Jones told his men: "We are now approaching the shore of California, the territory of Mexico, the enemy of our country, whose flag it is our duty to strike, and hoist in its place our own." The following afternoon, Jones' flagship the *United States* dropped anchor in the bay. Jones sent a message ashore to Governor Alvarado demanding the

surrender of the town and fort.

On the morning of the 20th, two Mexican ministers came aboard the *United States* to sign the surrender, and a party of 150 seamen and marines went ashore and raised the American flag over El Castillo on the hill overlooking the harbor. But the next day, after reading several recent newspapers that Larkin had in his possession, Jones realized his mistake. The two countries were not at war. He ordered the American flag taken down and the Mexican flag raised again in its place. He also extended his apologies to all. Alvarado and the Californios graciously accepted his apology and treated Jones and his crew to a feast and dancing. Then the American ships sailed south so that Jones could formally apologize to Governor Micheltorena in Santa Barbara.

Micheltorena was polite, but when news of the capture of Monterey reached Mexico City, the official response was outrage. Negotiations with Mexico for the United States' acquisition of California were summarily broken off. In response, Jones was recalled to Washington by the secretary of the navy. He was never tried in court and ultimately resumed his command of the Pacific squadron during the war with Mexico. But Jones' mistake in 1842 would weigh heavily on the mind of the earnest but cautious man who commanded the Pacific squadron in 1846 — Commodore John Drake Sloat.

Top, from left: Sailor, Muleteer, and Neophyte. Above, from left: Governor Portolá, Lt. Fages, and Ship's Captain.

Chapter 4

FROM SEA TO SHINING SEA

Sloat Takes Monterey

On July 2, 1846, and for several days after his arrival, Commodore Sloat met frequently with Thomas Oliver Larkin, the American consul in Monterey. Larkin was an amiable diplomat, who had dedicated considerable effort to bringing about the peaceful annexation of California by the United States. As a businessman, he saw the country's potential. As an American patriot, he longed to see California become part of the United States. He was confident, moreover, that the United States could offer his friends, the Californios, greater protection and more opportunity to shape their own destiny than was possible under Mexican rule.

In their first meetings, Larkin counseled Sloat to move slowly. He was disturbed by news from Sonoma that a band of Americans had taken over the town, imprisoned General Mariano Vallejo and announced the formation of an independent republic. He feared that such precipitous and belligerent action would turn the Californios away from the United States and lead to bloodshed.

Top: The Encampment of Company I, Camp Kearny, Monterey, April 1847, *as sketched in the daily journal of William Hollingsworth. Left: Thomas O. Larkin. Above: Raising the Stars and Stripes above the Monterey Custom House, July 7, 1846.*

Moreover, the news that U.S. Army Captain John C. Fremont was somehow involved with the "Bear Flag Revolt" puzzled both Larkin and Sloat. Sloat wondered whether Fremont was acting on his own or following orders. Both he and Larkin sent messengers to track down the captain, requesting that he come to Monterey as soon as possible. Meanwhile, Sloat worried that every day's delay would bring reprimands from his superiors; or worse, that the British would arrive and interfere with the execution of his orders.

On shore, rumors of an imminent American invasion flew from house to house along the streets of Monterey. Despite these anxieties, however, nearly 100 American crew men were allowed to spend 24 hours leave on July 3, and the town hosted a raucous party that carried over into the next day as the people of Monterey celebrated the day of Our Lady of Refuge with a fiesta. The Americans, with their ships dressed out in all their colors, celebrated the Fourth of July with a 21-gun salute.

Many citizens of Monterey believed that the Americans would take the town on July 4th, but still Sloat hesitated—hoping to learn that war had officially been declared between Mexico and the United States. Across the continent in Washington, D.C., the secretary of the navy believed the commodore had captured California weeks earlier. Meanwhile, in Sonoma, John Fremont and the other Bear Flag rebels celebrated Independence Day with fireworks and a reading of the Declaration of Independence.

Then on Sunday, July 5, Sloat was further confused by word from San Francisco that definitely confirmed Fremont's involvement with the Bear Flaggers. His own orders from the secretary of the navy stipulated that "you will be careful to preserve if possible the most friendly relations with the inhabitants (of California) and . . . will encourage them to adopt a course of neutrality." In contrast to these orders, Fremont was apparently engaged in belligerent combat. What Sloat did not know, was that Fremont was acting under his own orders and for the moment was AWOL from his command.

The next day Sloat summoned Larkin to a meeting on board the *Savannah*. "We must take the place!" he told the consul. "I shall be blamed for doing too little or too much—I prefer the latter." Larkin himself felt torn. He had hoped for too long that California would become part of the United States not to feel some measure of exhilaration. Yet, he would have preferred that the Californios had made the decision for themselves. But he conceded to Sloat that "the great Ball of Fate" had been rolled. "What can stop it?" he asked.

The two men spent much of the night drafting a summons demanding the military surrender of Monterey and California and issuing a proclamation to all Californians. The extraordinary proclamation reflected both Larkin and Sloat's concern for a peaceful and amicable transition of power.

> I declare to the inhabitants of California that, although I come in arms with a powerful force, I do not come among them as an enemy to California; on the contrary, I come as their best friend, as henceforward California will be a portion of the United States, and its peaceful inhabitants will enjoy the same rights and privileges they now enjoy, together with the privilege of choosing their own magistrates and other officers for the administration of justice among themselves; and the same protection will be extended to them as to any other state in the Union.

Sloat promised the Californians the same constitutional rights enjoyed by all Americans. Furthermore, he predicted that by joining the United States, the California economy would grow and all its inhabitants would prosper.

The next morning, July 7, at 7 a.m., an officer went ashore to deliver Sloat's demand for surrender to the military commandant of Monterey. The decks of the *Savannah* were cleared for action. An hour and a half later, Sloat received his reply. The artillery captain, Mariano Silva, stated that he had no authority to surrender Monterey, but that he would withdraw, leaving the town without a soldier.

At 10:20 a.m., 140 sailors and 85 marines under the command of Captain William Mervine landed at the wharf of the Custom House. Mervine read Sloat's proc-

lamation to the assembled crowd of American forces and citizens of Monterey. He had copies posted in both Spanish and English. A few moments later, the crowd watched as Mervine's men raised the American flag on the Custom House flagpole, symbolically linking the Pacific Coast with the Atlantic—one nation stretching from sea to shining sea. As the sailors and marines cheered, the cannons of the *Savannah* and the *Cyane* boomed a 21-gun salute that echoed and blew a cloud of blue smoke across the water.

Monterey Under American Rule

In the three years that followed Sloat's conquest, both Monterey and California as a whole experienced one drastic change after another. Within three weeks of his decision, Sloat turned over his command to the recently arrived Commodore Stockton, and sailed for home. For his part, Stockton declared that California had been "trifled with long enough" and officially constituted the "California battalion of United States troops" under the command of John Charles Fremont. Shortly thereafter, Fremont and the California Battalion headed south to subdue the rebellious Californios in the pueblo of Los Angeles. Stockton also appointed Walter Colton, the chaplain on board the *Congress,* as alcalde. Then, leaving Captain Mervine in charge of the military forces in Monterey, Stockton followed Fremont south in search of battle and glory.

Educated at Yale, Walter Colton was a judicious, personable and energetic man who soon became popular with all the various inhabitants of Monterey. Under Mexican law, which continued in effect under the watchful eye of the military commandant, the alcalde served as mayor, judge, and tax collector. Colton handled his position with delicacy and a lively sense of humor.

Describing Monterey during his first week on the job, Colton wrote: "Almost every nation has, in some emigrant, a representative here—a representative of its peculiar habits, virtues, and vices. Here is the reckless Californian, the half-wild Indian, the roving trapper of the West, the lawless Mexican, the licentious Spaniard, the scolding Englishman, the absconding Frenchman, the luckless Irishman, the plodding German, the adventurous Russian, and the discontented Mormon. All have come here with the expectation of finding but little work and less law. Through this discordant mass I am to maintain order, punish crime, and redress injuries."

In August, Colton and Robert Semple began publishing the *Californian* on a salvaged printing press. Fittingly, California's first newspaper was bilingual, printed in both Spanish and English. In its pages, Colton and Semple recorded the events of the war in the south as Fremont and Stockton, and later General Stephen Kearney, fought with the Californians and bickered with each other over who would govern California.

Commodore Sloat's ship, the Savannah, *painted by Hans Skalagard.*

CALIFORNIAN.

Vol. I   MONTEREY, SATURDAY, JANUARY 23, 1847.   No. 24.

The CALIFORNIAN—*Is published every Saturday morning.*
BY COLTON & SEMPLE.

Terms—SUBSCRIPTION, ONE YEAR IN DVANCE $5 00
"   SIX MONTHS   2 50
SINGLE COPIES,   12½

SIR ROBERT PEEL.

The New York Gazette has a graphic correspondent, who is writing a series of "Gallery Sketches of Public Characters," by an American in England. From one of his numbers we extract the following sketch of the Premier of Great Britain, Sir Robert Peel.

"This distinguished statesmen is in person rather above the common size, though not what might be termed, a large man—his complexion is light, and his hair what is called "sandy," his cheeks full, which diminish the size of his mouth and eyes. At first glance a stranger would not pronounce him a man of intellect or genius—but it is only necessary to attend one debate in the House of Commons, on which the Premier takes a part, to be convinced that he is not only a man of extraordinary powers, but far superior to any other member on that floor—in fact, although I have been present on many occasions, and sat for hours at a time, in listening to every variety of debate there, I never witnessed an instance where the most powerful, on "the opposition benches," no matter on what subject, with or without notice, did not find his overmatch in Sir Robert, or the Rt. Honorable Baronet, as they term him. His manner is remarkably easy, his tone of voice soft and agreeable, and he is entirely free from the habit of hesitation, and repetition, and "mumbling," which is so peculiar to the English. In this respect he *almost* equals the best American speakers in fluency; but there is no violence or heat, his object seems to be first to convince and next to persuade in the most amiable way. I suppose I have heard him speak at least fifty times, and never recollect witnessing in his manner a loss of temper; he was always gentlemanly and courteous, as if he felt his position and power, he required no other means to carry his object, or that long experience had taught him that they were the most efficient means. As I am in the habit of tracing resemblances, I should say that a person familiar with the appearance of Col. Benton of the United States Senate, would at first be struck with his resemblance to Sir Robert Peel; whilst the voice and manner of the latter, closely resemble that of the late Mr. Biddle of Philadelphia.

After becoming somewhat acquainted with the political history of the Premier, and informed of the peculiar relation he bears to the great contending parties of the day, it is peculiarly interesting to watch and notice on all occasions the consummate skill he manifests in keeping himself in that position which enables him to steer his way through old prejudices long established, and new theories and systems of modern origin—or in other words to keep "Old England" in harmony with "Young England"—and to draw from both the best material to construct his "Political Pantheon"—and hence it is that on almost every occasion touching matters of public interest, his remarks are alternately interrupted by the cry of "hear"—"hear" from the "Tory," the "Whig" and "Conservative" circles. Each being able to recognize some material in the structure; drawn from his own laboratory: and so he proceeds in building up what I term a "Political Pantheon," and which, when finished, will, like that of Rome, be spared perhaps longer than another even by Goth and Vandal; fearing that in its demolition they may destroy a portion of their own art and handy work. He has in fact been

conducting a revolution in England so quietly and adroitly, that the most of them are unconscious of the changes he has produced, except by their benefits.

There was a capital caricature of him in Punch, a short time ago, in which he is represented as the 'man what plays on many instruments.' there was as much truth as wit in this, for with ... ion on the mind, one can't listen to h... te without being under the pers... he harmonious flourishes of ... ic, the cheering notes o'... tannin rules the Wave ... nd" (they won't sa... it is also that "Ol... power or will to s... onise its parts so ...

There ... not fail to strik ... bench, and nea ... s of the Govern ... n mere look fro ... reply to some en ... the "opposite sid ... ll trained to take th ... all courteous, and ... hem as the "soft fender... e Thames, at the numerous ... and other objects of contact ... prevent an injurious thump or sc... the approach and according to the exten... ger he interposes the "fender" necessary to protect his boat, (for he has fenders of all sizes at hand,) but when there is a strong current, a high wind or any other great occasion, he uses himself, the greatest and most re... "the Queen" has on board; and no ma... k may be threatened, the contact ... injury, unless he happens to p... r against the assailant: b... ers are generally smo...

The m... the labors of his of... h for the mental ... roved so to man ... rk well, and is ... nan and has giv... ccasion, so that ... my personal l... reports) that w... ke," (as Wellin... lickor y of his d... however necessar... s for little unless co... e.

Take hi ... , perhaps, one of the ... and not the least of his hi ... estimate of our country; and I ... indulging in a narrow satisfaction... contrasting our late financial mishaps, he ... proper occasions expresses deep regret, and feeling a just pride in our common origin, laws, language and habits, is never more gratified than in evidences of our prosperity and advancement. I have this assurance from the very best authority, and it gives me pleasure to record it in this my hurried *sketch* of the "Premier of England."

*Robert Semple (top) and Walter Colton (above) started
California's first newspaper,* The Californian, *in 1846.*

*Above: The old Monterey jail.
Below: "The whole country, from
San Francisco to Los Angeles, and
from the seashore to the base of the
Sierra Nevadas, resounds with the
sordid cry of 'gold, Gold, GOLD!'
while the field is left half-planted,
the house half-built, and everything
neglected but the manufacture of
shovels and pickaxes." From the
San Francisco* Californian, *May 29,
1848. Opposite: Colton Hall today.*

In March 1847, under orders from the secretary of war, Kearney assumed command of civil and military affairs with his base in Monterey. But at the very same time, in Southern California, Fremont asserted his authority as governor of California by virtue of his appointment by Commodore Stockton. Eventually, Kearney would have Fremont arrested for mutiny and insubordination and Fremont would be court-martialed in Washington, D.C. To many Californio and Indian citizens of Monterey, however, this north-south struggle for authority was hardly news. The Americans seemed little different from their Mexican predecessors.

In other ways, however, the Americans brought tremendous changes. In addition to publishing California's first newspaper, Colton impaneled the first American jury ever organized on the West Coast: one third Mexican, one third Californian, and one third American. Under Mexican law, there had been two forms of criminal punishment: fines for persons of Spanish-Mexican descent and whippings for Indians. Colton put criminal offenders to work making adobes and building public facilities including California's first schoolhouse and town meeting place—Colton Hall.

The Mexican-American war ended on February 2, 1848, with the signing of the Treaty of Guadalupe-Hidalgo. Upper California was officially a permanent part of the United States. Just nine days earlier, unbeknownst to anyone in Mexico, James Marshall had discovered gold in the American River near Sacramento. Suddenly, California was infinitely more valuable than anyone had imagined.

For the Californios the discovery of gold was ultimately much more of a disaster than the American conquest. If Larkin and Vallejo and others had dreamed of a gradual transition to American rule and a blending of the best of Californio and American ways of life, all those hopes were crushed by the massive influx of gold seekers.

Within two years, some 50,000 newly arrived fortune hunters overran the state. In 1848, however, "Golden Yellow Fever," as it was called by Thomas Oliver Larkin, reduced Monterey and San Francisco to virtual ghost towns. Larkin lamented that "Every bowl, tray, and warming pan has gone to the mines. Everything in short that has a scoop in it and will hold sand and water." Walter Colton wrote that the gold mines had upset all social and domestic arrangements in Monterey, making the master his own servant and the servant his own lord as, one by one, individuals returned from the mines with thousands of dollars in gold dust and nuggets.

For the American military governors of California based in Monterey, the first 18 months after the end of the war and the discovery of gold presented a series of trials and tribulations. In peacetime, they had no legitimate authority to govern. By all rights, Congress should have immediately established some form of representative government for California either as a state or as a territory. But Congress was fiercely divided over the issue of slavery and would not make any decisions about California for fear of upsetting the delicate balance between slave states and free states.

In the absence of direction from Congress, a succession of American military officers attempted to govern the rapidly changing countryside as best they could. But soldiers and sailors deserted for the mines as fast as servants and vaqueros. Miners could scoop up more in a day than soldiers could earn in a year.

When Congress adjourned in 1849 without making any decisions about California, military governor General Bennett Riley decided to force the issue by calling for a constitutional convention to be held in Monterey in September. The delegates came from all over California and were amazingly representative of the whole population: seven were Californios including Mariano Vallejo, Antonio Pico, and José Antonio Carrillo; six others had lived in California for more than a decade including Thomas Abel Stearns and Oliver Larkin, John Sutter, Robert Semple. Thirteen newcomers had resided in California less than a year. Nine of the delegates were under 30 years old and 14 were lawyers. The convention was conducted in both Spanish and English and was open to the public. Among the spectators were John C. and Jessie Fremont, Lieutenant William T. Sherman, and a reporter from the *New York Tribune* named Bayard Taylor.

For six weeks the delegates met in Colton Hall and debated the framework of a constitution for the proposed state of California. The document they framed, among other things, outlawed slavery, set the state's boundaries, recognized the separate property rights of wives, set punishments for crimes, banned state lotteries, and provided that all the state's documents would be published in Spanish and English. Much to the dismay of the citizens of Monterey, the delegates also voted to move the capital to San Jose.

When they were done, the delegates contributed $25 each to sponsor a ball for the people of Monterey, and on the evening of the 12th of October; 60 or 70 women and as many men crowded into Colton Hall to dance and celebrate. At three o'clock the next afternoon, the delegates put their signatures on the final draft of the constitution. A month later the voters of California ratified the document, and in December, the state legislature met in San Jose (the new capital) and began to govern, despite the fact that Congress had still not admitted California as a state.

Within weeks, Monterey's 75-year tenure as the capital of California came to an end. Largely forgotten, the scattered descendants of the Ohlone gathered into one community near the edge of town and began a new way of life that blended their traditions and the ways of the Spanish and Mexicans.

Many Californios and most of the Americans and other foreigners left Monterey soon after the constitutional convention, moving to the burgeoning gold rush city of San Francisco. In the next few decades, as the locus for politics and commerce on the Pacific Coast moved northward Monterey was largely forgotten by the world at large.

Opposite, top: Walter Colton (inset) and the signed constitutional convention agreement of September 1849. Above: Colton Hall interior. The room in which the constitutional convention was held. Middle right: The great seal of California. Bottom: Colton Hall as it looked during the late 1800s.

Chapter 5

A REFUGE FOR ARTISTS, A RESORT FOR THE RICH,

Cannery Row, and a Living Past

The one common note of all this country is the haunting presence of the ocean...the roar of water dwells in the clean, empty rooms of Monterey as in a shell upon the chimney....

—Robert Louis Stevenson
The Old Pacific Capital, 1880

In the decades that followed the constitutional convention, the course of history seemed to leave Monterey further and further behind. Even in the late 19th century, if the old Pacific capital was celebrated at all, it was for its peace and quiet, its atmosphere of bygone days. A promotional tract written in the 1870s claimed that "a worn-out invalid, or a man whose brains have been racked with toil" would find that "the magnetic influence of the atmosphere grants him sleep and restful health."

In August 1879, when writer Robert Louis Stevenson stepped off the Monterey and Salinas Valley Railroad after traveling half-way round the world to be with the woman he loved, the sleepy village of Monterey had less than 400 residents. Fishing and agriculture were the primary sources of income. Portuguese whalers, who worked the coast of California, made Monterey their home and headquarters. Beyond the small train depot a dusty road led into town.

Above: Alvarado St. in the late 1800s. Left: Robert Louis Stevenson. Opposite, top: Chinese fishermen near Point Cabrillo in Monterey about 1875. Right: Portuguese whalers on the California coast worked out of Monterey in the late 19th and early 20th centuries.

"Chinese Fishermen"
Monterey, California. 187_
© Dresler

Stevenson remained in Monterey for three and a half months, waiting for Mrs. Fanny Osbourne to divorce her husband. The two had met at an artists' retreat in Europe. Estranged from her husband, Fanny had fallen in love with the young writer, but eventually returned to California. They continued to exchange letters, however, and it was after receiving a particularly alarming letter from Fanny that Stevenson had booked passage to America to join her. On the voyage and during his trip across country he became extremely ill. He arrived in Monterey exhausted and near death.

But Fanny could not openly receive him. Stevenson was befriended by Jules Simoneau, the owner of a local restaurant, who helped him find a room in what was then called the French Hotel. Stevenson ate his one meal a day in Simoneau's restaurant. When he could, the young writer socialized with Fanny and her San Francisco artist friends, who increasingly saw Monterey as an ideal retreat from the big city.

While he waited for Fanny, Stevenson worked on stories and wrote articles for the Monterey newspaper. He spent so much time wandering along the beaches and through the forest that the locals called him "Beachcomber." In his writings, Stevenson captured the essence of old Monterey at a time when it was on the verge of vast change.

Scarcely four months after Stevenson left Monterey to join Fanny in San Francisco, where the two of them eventually married, the magnificent Hotel Del Monte opened in Monterey and transformed the town from a backwater into an international destination point. Established by Charles Crocker and served by his Southern Pacific Railroad, the Del Monte was the first of California's grand resort hotels. Surrounded by a park of 126 acres, the hotel could accommodate 750 guests. Its owners called it "The Queen of American Watering Places."

Seven years later, at midnight on April 1,1887, a fire broke out that destroyed the hotel in an hour. Undaunted, Charles Crocker quickly rebuilt on an even more lavish scale. In the 1890s, he added a golf course. Guests rode in horsedrawn carriages along the scenic Seventeen Mile Drive from the hotel, around the tip of the peninsula, and back through the coastal forest. And despite another fire in the 1920s, the hotel continued to thrive until the Depression.

Opposite: The California First
Theater about 1890. An English
sailor by the name of Jack Swan
(left) constructed this building
during the 1840s and used it mainly
as a saloon and boarding house for
seafaring men. Above: The original
Del Monte Hotel, built in 1880.
Right: A vintage map of the Monterey
Peninsula and its world-famous
17-mile drive. Below: Stevenson's
good friend Jules Simoneau outside
his restaurant at the intersection of
Pearl and Munras streets.

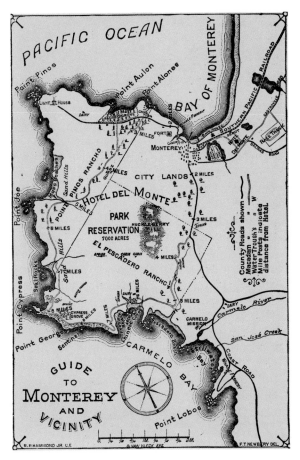

Left: Booth's Cannery at the turn of the century. Above: Through his best-selling novels, Cannery Row *and* Sweet Thursday, *John Steinbeck made* Cannery Row *world-famous. Below: Steinbeck's close friend and mentor, marine biologist Edward F. Ricketts. Opposite: Fisherman's Wharf in the 1950s.*

In spite of the Del Monte's success, however, Monterey's economy did not really begin to expand until the early 1900s, when Frank E. Booth began experimenting with canning sardines. The small fish flourished in and around Monterey Bay and Booth hoped to sell them commercially. With the help of a young Norwegian named Knute Hovden and a Sicilian fisherman, Pietro Ferrante, the sardine operation eventually grew into a multimillion dollar business.

By 1913, the local fishermen, many of Italian descent and recruited by Ferrante, were catching 25 tons of sardines a night. By 1918, nine canneries were packing 1.4 million cases of sardines each year and Monterey was the "Sardine Capital of the World."

By the early 1950s, the sardines had been fished out, and the canneries went out of business. Even as the industry began to decline, however, the canneries and the people who worked in and around them were fixed in the imagination of millions of Americans by a writer named John Steinbeck.

Growing up in nearby Salinas, Steinbeck lived in Monterey during the Depression. Years later, he wrote about the people he knew on what he dubbed Cannery Row, including his good friend, marine biologist Edward Ricketts. In his books, *Cannery Row* and *Sweet Thursday,* Steinbeck used a unique blend of humor and seriousness to describe life on the Monterey waterfront. Eventually, his stories helped rejuvenate the tourist industry, which in the late 19th and early 20th centuries had been so crucial to Monterey's economy.

In 1942, the United States government leased the Del Monte Hotel, whose days as a resort were all but over, and turned it into the Naval Postgraduate School. The school became part of a complex of Monterey County military installations that included Fort Ord and the Army Language School (now the Defense Language Institute) on the hill above the old Spanish fortress, El Castillo. During World War II, these institutions dominated life in Monterey as military personnel moved in and out of the area. They continue to play an important part in the character and economy of the city.

Today, Monterey is once again world-renowned as a resort community and a haven for the arts. Each year the city plays host to the Monterey Jazz Festival, the Dixieland Festival, the Blues Festival, and a number of other special musical and cultural events.

Reminders of the native people who once gathered abalone, mussels, and a wide variety of other seafood from the waters of the bay can still be found. The Spanish settlers, soldiers, and missionaries who built the chapel and the old presidio have left their mark as well. In fact, more than 50 historic buildings remain—many of them the adobe homes of Californios who worked, ate, sang, and danced at the edge of the New World just before the Industrial Revolution and worldwide political events completely and permanently changed human experience in California and throughout the American West.

Today, the remnants of old Monterey offer a unique opportunity to look back at a time and place where the large currents of world history focused sharply for a moment—a place where an ancient Indian way of life was torn apart by the convulsive, northernmost push of the dying Spanish Empire, a provincial capital where Spanish and Mexican governors lived and worked for nearly eight decades, and the site of Alta California's provincial capital from 1775 to 1846. While enjoying Monterey's gentle climate, its beautiful setting, and many contemporary attractions, it is also possible to seek out the exact place, to put your hand on the flag-pole, where the Stars and Stripes were first raised on the west coast of North America, the place where the great American dream of Manifest Destiny became a reality. You can also walk into the building, into the very room, where the modern state of California was created through the difficult and demanding democratic process of a constitutional convention.

This kind of historical exploration can be especially rewarding in downtown Monterey today because just behind and beyond the bustle of contemporary life, it is still possible to discover old Monterey—California's forgotten first capital.

The Serra Monument, a gift of Jane L. Stanford in 1891, stands on the hill above Lighthouse Point overlooking the site of Serra's landing in 1770.

HISTORICAL PRESERVATION IN MONTEREY

Monterey's historical preservation movement began in the 1880s when the Native Sons of the Golden West first attempted to have the Monterey Custom House designated as a historical landmark. This effort was blocked for more than a decade by local political and commercial interests, but in 1900 the Native Sons succeeded in leasing the Custom House property from the federal government. They took steps to protect the building from weather and vandals, and in 1901 persuaded the State of California to take over the lease and appropriate state funds for preservation and restoration work.

The state established a Custom House board of trustees to look after the Custom House and later assigned this same group the responsibility of caring for other nearby historic buildings. Preliminary restoration work on the Custom House was completed by the State of California in 1903 and the building was formally designated a historical landmark. Today, it is California's State Historic Landmark Number One. At the urging of the Native Sons and other private groups and individuals, further restoration work was carried out with state funds in 1917, and in 1938, 11 citizens of Monterey contributed the private matching funds that enabled the California State Park System to purchase the Custom House and its surrounding land from the federal government.

This building houses the Allen Knight Maritime Muse

Casa del Oro.

The Cooper-Molera Complex during restoration in the early 1980s.

Meanwhile, in 1906, the California Landmarks League acquired California's First Theater and donated it to the state. It was administered by the Custom House Board of Trustees until 1929 and then turned over to the newly created California Division of Parks for inclusion in the California State Park System. Today, Monterey State Historic Park is made up of 17 buildings and sites, including the Custom House, First Theater, Pacific House, Casa del Oro, the Soberanes Adobe, Robert Louis Stevenson House, the Old Whaling Station, First Brick House, the Alvarado Adobe, the Gutierrez Adobe, and Larkin House. The Department has also restored and is operating the Cooper-Molera Complex.

Today, private citizens and volunteer organizations are continuing Monterey's proud tradition of active private-sector involvement in historical preservation and interpretation.

The Old Monterey Preservation Society, for example, is a non-profit, cooperative association designed to work closely with Monterey State Historic Park. They provide docent services, operate and staff the Cooper Store, where unusual gifts and books pertinent to Monterey's history may be purchased, and put on special events such as the annual open house, "Christmas in the Adobes." They also present slide programs, living history programs, and craft demonstrations, as well as special interpretive events.

The Junior League of Monterey County has taken the lead responsibility for operating, furnishing, and interpreting Monterey's Old Whaling Station and First Brick House.

The California Heritage Guide Service provides an information service and trained guides for tours of Monterey, Monterey State Historic Park, and the Monterey Peninsula in general.

The Community Foundation of Monterey County has been helpful at crucial moments in terms of supporting various historical preservation efforts.

The largest and oldest of Monterey's non-profit historical preservation organizations is the Monterey History and Art Association, which was incorporated in January 1931. This is the organization that created Monterey's historic landmark program and laid out Monterey's first Path of History. In cooperation with the City of Monterey, the association co-sponsors several of the city's major annual celebrations, including "The Merienda," the "Sloat Landing Commemoration," and the "Adobe Tour." The association owns and maintains several historic buildings: Casa Serrano, Fremont Headquarters, the Francis Doud House, and St. James Church. It also maintains several historical collections, including the paintings, prints, model ships, and other artifacts in the Allen Knight Maritime Museum.

The U.S. Army owns the site of El Castillo as well as the Sloat Monument. The site of the original Presidio de Monterey is owned by the Catholic Church, which continues to use the Royal Presidio Chapel as an active place of worship.

The City of Monterey owns and maintains the Old Monterey Jail and Colton Hall. In fact, Colton Hall's large upstairs room in which the constitutional convention was held in 1849 is now a museum exhibit operated by the staff and volunteers associated with the Colton Hall Museum. The city also maintains the Path of History and co-sponsors various annual events, including a unique, living-history presentation about the constitutional convention.

Opposite, top: California's First Theater today. Opposite, below: Colton Hall today. Top to bottom: The First Brick House in California as it looked in 1875; the old Whaling Station in 1875; Casa Serrano in the 1950s.

THE PAST AS IT CAN BE SEEN TODAY

In this age of sprawling and impersonal mega-cities, Monterey remains intimate, compact, and recognizable within its natural geographic boundaries: the curving shoreline of the bay, the inland waters of El Estero, the gentle promontory of Lighthouse Point, and behind the town, a protective rim of hills covered with pine forest. Even the streets of downtown Monterey (despite the best efforts of several generations of modern surveyors, traffic engineers, and paving contractors) still reflect the spontaneous, informal, and sometimes personal decisions of Spanish and Mexican Monterey.

All this is quickly apparent to anyone who drives or walks through the downtown area, or views the city from the air or any high place. Less apparent is that many of Monterey's Spanish and Mexican Period adobes have been preserved and still stand, shoulder to shoulder with newer and larger buildings, throughout the downtown area. In fact, many of Monterey's most important historic buildings are owned by public agencies or by non-profit organizations that are dedicated to preserving the buildings and keeping them open to the public.

These old buildings are a magnificent educational

resource in our time and provide a new perspective on our contemporary experience. They remind us that other people have lived very different lives right here in places that we can see, touch, smell, and even walk through today.

Enter one of Monterey's old adobes, look around, and perhaps rest your hand on a cool, white wall and it is only natural to wonder about the many human events, great and small, that have occurred in the space you have entered. Put a finger to a rough-cut, hand-hewn timber or the uneven surface of an adobe wall and you can almost feel the hand of the Indian or Mexican laborer at work on the building you are in.

Ohlone hunters and gatherers, 18th and 19th century Spanish soldiers, Yankee sailors and merchants, mountain men with their beaver traps and long rifles, 19th-century American sailors and settlers, and Californios of all kinds (politicians, customs officials, missionaries, rancheros, vaqueros, shopkeepers, servants, and ladies young and old in splendid silks) have known these buildings, have hoped and dreamed and worried, fought, made peace, danced, laughed, and made love here.

Today, the old **Monterey Custom House** is filled with the kind of trade goods that were typical of ship's cargoes during the 1830s. Outside, at the north end of the building, the flagpole still stands in the very place where Commodore John Drake Sloat's men raised the Stars and Stripes on July 7, 1846, and made the United States of America into a continental nation.

In a small ravine just a little to the northeast, a **monument** commemorates the landing place of Sebastián Vizcaíno in 1602 and the even more momentous arrival of Captain Gaspar de Portolá and Father Serra in 1770. On the hill above Lighthouse Avenue, the site of **El Castillo** is still an excellent place to look over the harbor, Fisherman's Wharf, and the whole town of Monterey. Farther up the hill, the **Sloat Monument** provides an even larger vista of land and sea.

Countless generations of people have enjoyed this vista. We can be sure of that because we know that, for at least 15 or 20 centuries, a large **Indian village** was located in the lee of this hill. Other Indian villages and signs of occupation have also been located in the vicinity of Monterey.

The original Spanish presidio established in 1770 near El Estero has largely disappeared over the years,

45

Left: The Royal Presidio Chapel today. From the day in 1791 when this chapel was completed, the little red lamp in the sanctuary has never ceased to burn, a symbol of life everlasting. Above: The new "Monterey Style" of architecture introduced by Larkin in his house in the 1830s. Below, left: Cooper-Molera Complex exterior. Below: Cooper-Molera interior.

though the **Royal Presidio Chapel** (completed in 1795) is still in good condition and is still an active place of worship. The mother of the California missions, Father Serra's beloved **Mission San Carlos Borroméo,** remains where Father Serra moved it in 1771 — over the hill to the south, close behind the mouth of the Carmel River.

Monterey began to expand beyond the walls of the old presidio during the 1820s and many of Monterey's oldest adobe buildings therefore date from the 1820s and 1830s. The **Cooper-Molera Complex** features exhibits about Juan Bautista Cooper and life in Monterey during the Mexican period of California history. A little bookstore and gift shop is open daily from 10 a.m. to 4 or 5 p.m. (except Wednesdays) and makes this a good place to start your tour of old Monterey.

The **Larkin House** is beautifully furnished with Larkin's desk, photographs, and personal memorabilia as well as the china, glassware, and other antique furnishings of Larkin's granddaughter, who donated the house to the California Department of Parks and Recreation in 1957.

Pacific House, Casa del Oro, California's First Theater, and other buildings near the Custom House Plaza all relate primarily to the story of the American takeover in 1846 and afterwards. Pacific House serves as a visitor center, another good place to start your tour of old Monterey. It features exhibits about the whole story of Monterey and of American Indian life before the coming of Europeans.

Top: Larkin House is beautifully preserved and features furniture belonging to the Larkins. Above: Thomas Larkin's desk.

Quartel House, Monterey, California. 1875

Colton Hall is still used for public purposes just as Walter Colton envisioned it in the 1840s when he served as the first alcalde under U.S. military rule. The second floor room where the constitutional convention was held has been restored to its 1849 appearance when 50 young men gathered in Monterey to draft, debate, and finally adopt a constitution for the proposed state of California.

The old adobe rooming house that Robert Louis Stevenson lived in during his stay in Monterey in 1879 has been thoroughly restored and now houses a fine collection of Stevenson's personal possessions and memorabilia of the time. Unfortunately, a stone's throw from **Stevenson House,** a pair of automobile service stations now stand on the site of **El Cuartel,** the long, narrow adobe building that was the capitol of Alta California from 1840 to 1850.

Many of Monterey's other old adobes have survived and can be seen in the downtown area. A self-guiding "Path of History" publication is available to help visitors discover and enjoy the remains of old Monterey — California's forgotten first capital.

A combination of historical overtones and lively present-day activities (hotels, restaurants, shops, and museums) attract many visitors to **Fisherman's Wharf** and also to **Cannery Row,** which John Steinbeck immortalized in his novels, *Cannery Row* and *Sweet Thursday.* The **Monterey Bay Aquarium,** now a leading attraction in the area, has been built on the site of and within the space originally occupied by the Hovden Cannery. Other new buildings within the area also reflect the architectural heritage of Cannery Row.

A few blocks away from these very popular waterfront attractions, the grand buildings and spacious grounds of the once world-famous **Del Monte Hotel** are now the home of the U.S. Naval Postgraduate School. The public is welcome to visit the site between 6 a.m. and 6 p.m. and tours can be arranged by contacting the school's public affairs office.

Top: El Cuartel as it appeared in 1875. This building faced Munras Avenue just south of Jules Simoneau Plaza. It was the capitol of Mexican California from 1840 to 1846; the U.S. military governors of California headquartered here from 1846 to 1850. Above: Stevenson House today. Below: The shops and restaurants of Fisherman's Wharf are still a popular tourist destination.